Who Was
Sally Ride?

by Megan Stine

illustrated by Ted Hammond

Penguin Workshop

For Maddy, Travis, and Daryl, who all know how to reach for the stars—MS

To Mom—TH

PENGUIN WORKSHOP
An Imprint of Penguin Random House LLC, New York

Text copyright © 2013 by Megan Stine. Illustrations copyright © 2013 by Ted Hammond. Cover illustration copyright © 2013 by Penguin Random House LLC. All rights reserved. Published by Penguin Workshop, an imprint of Penguin Random House LLC, New York. PENGUIN and PENGUIN WORKSHOP are trademarks of Penguin Books Ltd. WHO HQ & Design is a registered trademark of Penguin Random House LLC. Printed in the USA.

Visit us online at www.penguinrandomhouse.com.

Library of Congress Control Number: 2013938724

ISBN 9780448466873   20 19

Contents

Who Was Sally Ride?..1

As Good as the Boys..5

A Major Choice..16

Help Wanted: Astronauts......................................22

Five Years of Hard Work......................................35

Liftoff!...50

Being Sally Ride..76

Tragedy in Space...83

Starting Over...91

Science Is for Girls..95

Timelines...102

Bibliography...105

Who Was
Sally Ride?

One day in 1977, Sally Ride walked across the campus of her college and picked up a school newspaper. She flipped through the pages and scanned the job ads. All of a sudden, she saw something incredible! The US space program was looking for new astronauts. And for the first time ever they were encouraging women to apply.

Sally had been in college for eight long years at that point. Studying hard, she had already earned three degrees. Soon she would graduate with her fourth degree, in physics. She was planning to be a scientist and a college professor.

It had never occurred to Sally to be an astronaut. However, the minute she saw that ad, she knew she wanted to apply. She sent in her application that very same day. Even though she had never flown a plane, she believed she could do the job.

More than eight thousand men and women from all over the country answered the ad. But NASA—the National Aeronautics and Space Administration—only needed thirty-five new astronauts. Would Sally be one of them?

Yes! In January 1978, she got a phone call from an official at NASA, asking if she still wanted the job.

"Yes, sir!" she said right away.

Normally Sally was calm and levelheaded. But when she called her mother with the news, she was almost breathless. How could she be calm about something as exciting as this? She was going to be an astronaut! And although she didn't know it yet, she was going to be the first American woman in space.

Chapter 1
As Good as the Boys

Sally Kristen Ride was born on May 26, 1951, in Encino, California.

Her parents were both teachers. Her father, Dale Ride, was a college professor. Her mother, Joyce Ride, had taught full-time before Sally was born. After that, Joyce Ride stayed home to take care of her children. But Joyce also worked at her church, taught English to foreign students, and was a counselor in a women's jail.

Two years after Sally was born, her baby sister, Karen, came along. Sally couldn't pronounce "Karen" so she called her "Bear." The name stuck! Even as a grown-up, Karen was called Bear Ride by everyone who knew her.

The house Sally grew up in was filled with

books, and Sally read everything—Nancy Drew
mysteries, *Mad* magazine, James Bond spy novels,
science fiction, and grown-up science magazines.

She even read a book called *Danny Dunn and the Anti-Gravity Paint!* From the age of five, she also read the newspaper. Her favorite section was the sports page. She knew the baseball statistics by heart.

Reading was a great indoor activity, but Sally loved being outdoors most of all. Whenever she

could, she went out to play football or baseball with the neighborhood boys. And the boys were happy to have her. Why not? She was better than most of them! In fact, Sally was usually picked first for the team.

When she was young, Sally thought she would grow up to be a quarterback for the University of California, Los Angeles, Bruins. Or maybe a shortstop for the Dodgers. She didn't think anything would stop her. She believed a girl could do anything.

When Sally turned nine, her parents decided to go on a family adventure. Her father took a year off from teaching so they could travel together in Europe. For a while, they lived in Yugoslavia and had a dog there as a pet. Joyce and Dale Ride

tutored the girls during the trip, to make sure Sally and Bear kept up with their subjects. But they also believed that traveling and seeing the world was just as important as school.

Sally's parents were right. When they came home to California, Sally was ahead of the other students her age. She skipped a grade in school that fall, making her the youngest in her class. Sally was quiet and shy in school. But she was a good student, especially when she liked the subject. Both at school and at home, she liked science. Her family had a telescope and a toy chemistry set that she enjoyed.

Sports were still Sally's favorite activities, though. Back home in the US, her parents bought her a tennis racket. Playing tennis seemed safer to them than letting her play football in the middle of the street!

Sally wasn't just good at tennis. She was great! Pretty soon she was taking lessons from Alice

Marble, a famous tennis champion. Alice Marble's students were among the best young tennis players in the country. By the time she was twelve, Sally was playing in national junior tennis matches all over the country. Many of the other players would become professionals.

At the same time, she met another tennis player—a girl her age named Tam O'Shaughnessy. Tam was also a tennis star—even better than Sally! Tam and Sally would be friends for the rest of their lives.

Because of her tennis skills, Sally won a scholarship to a private high school. The Westlake School for Girls was near Beverly Hills. Some of Sally's new classmates were the daughters of famous Hollywood actors. But that wasn't what Sally liked about her school. She loved two things: playing tennis and studying science. She not only played on the Westlake team, but she often played tennis against the head of the school—and beat him!

Sally had always been good at science. But her real love of science kicked in at Westlake. Her eleventh grade science teacher—Dr. Elizabeth Mommaerts—was the reason.

Dr. Mommaerts taught Sally about using reason and logic to solve problems in science. Sally loved the way Dr. Mommaerts's mind worked. The two of them hit it off right away and became close friends. Sadly, by the time Sally was chosen to be an astronaut, Dr. Mommaerts had died. Sally wished she could have shared the amazing news with her beloved teacher.

Chapter 2
A Major Choice

After high school, Sally headed off to
Swarthmore College in Pennsylvania. Swarthmore
was a great school—but it was a long way
from home. There was another problem with
Swarthmore—the weather. With cold winters

and no indoor tennis courts, Sally could only play tennis a few months of the school year.

In her freshman and sophomore years, Sally won a major tennis championship for Swarthmore. She beat all the best women players at other colleges in the East. Her tennis game was getting better all the time.

Sally started to wonder: Was college what she really wanted to do? Or should she try to become a pro tennis player instead?

She decided that she had to give tennis a real try. In the middle of her sophomore year, she dropped out of college and went home. Her parents weren't too happy, but they had always let Sally follow her dreams.

Sally plunged into playing tennis full-time. She did take a few college classes at the University of California, Los Angeles, though. Billie Jean King was the most famous female tennis champion at the time. She saw Sally play and was impressed. She told Sally to give up college altogether and go after a tennis career.

But after a while, Sally realized that although she was very good, she wasn't great. She would never be a world-class champion—and Sally wanted to be excellent at everything she did.

Sally decided to go back to college and follow her other great interest—science. Instead of returning to Swarthmore, though, she enrolled at Stanford University. Stanford was in sunny California, where the weather was perfect for tennis, and Sally was closer to home. Both made Sally happier.

At Stanford, Sally majored in physics, the science that studies how the physical world works. She also took a lot of math classes, played tennis, ran five miles a day, and played rugby.

One of Sally's friends was an English major, so Sally decided to try an English class. To her surprise, she loved it! She especially liked Shakespeare. Reading Shakespeare's plays was like solving a puzzle to her. You had to figure out what the words in the speeches meant, and then find clues to prove that you were right.

By the time she graduated from Stanford, Sally had earned two degrees—one in English and one in physics. But she wasn't finished with her studies. She stayed on at Stanford four and a half more years. She studied the X-rays given off by stars.

Finally, in 1977, she was ready to get her PhD. She was going to be Dr. Sally Ride—not a medical doctor but an astrophysicist! That's the name for a scientist who studies the properties of things in space, such as what stars are made of.

But even an astrophysicist needs a job. What kind of job would Sally find? Sally opened up the school newspaper and started reading the job ads.

Chapter 3
Help Wanted: Astronauts

When the space program started in the late 1950s, there were only seven astronauts. They were all military test pilots who tried out the newest and fastest planes being made. Choosing pilots as astronauts made sense in the early days

Gus Grissom

Alan Shepard

Gordon Cooper

Wally Schirra

Deke Slayton

John Glenn

Scott Carpe

of the space program. For one thing, nobody had ever flown in space before 1961. Space travel seemed dangerous. NASA wanted pilots who were used to dangerous missions. For another thing, the first space capsules were so tiny, there was no room for extra passengers. Every astronaut had to be a pilot.

But by 1977, things had changed. NASA had sent more than twenty men to the moon. More

spaceflights were taking place each year. And now NASA was planning to build a new kind of spacecraft—the space shuttle. It would be much bigger than the old space capsules—big enough to carry five, six, or maybe even seven astronauts at a time.

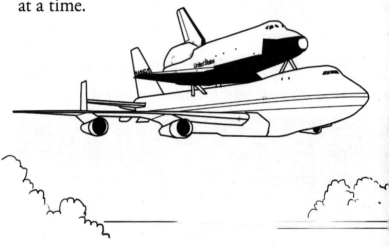

This meant that scientists, doctors, and engineers could go into space—not just pilots. Scientists could find out how space affected all living things. Engineers could help launch satellites into space. Satellites are pieces of equipment that circle around the Earth. Some of them take pictures of Earth's weather. Others send back TV, radio, and telephone signals to Earth.

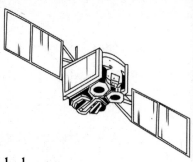

To do this work, NASA needed more astronauts for the space-shuttle program.

And thanks to the women's movement, everyone at NASA knew it was time to include women in the job.

NASA ran the ad for astronauts in dozens of college newspapers across the country. Sally wasn't the only person from Stanford who applied. So did a lot of her friends!

Out of more than 8,000 applications, about 6,500 were from men and 1,500 were from women. NASA read each person's application.

STANFORD DAII

Applicants Wanted for NASA Space Program

By October 1977 they had decided to interview 208 people.

Sally Ride was one of them!

That month, Sally flew to the Johnson Space Center in Houston, Texas, where NASA's had its headquarters.

There Sally saw how unusual it was for women to be part of the space program. In a later interview, she estimated there were 4,000 people working in science and technology jobs in Houston—only four of them were women!

THE WOMEN'S MOVEMENT

IN THE 1950S—WHEN SALLY RIDE WAS GROWING UP—MOST WOMEN DIDN'T HAVE PAYING JOBS. THEY STAYED AT HOME AND TOOK CARE OF THEIR CHILDREN, OR THEY HELD JOBS THAT WERE THOUGHT OF AS WOMEN'S JOBS: TEACHERS, SECRETARIES, AND NURSES. MEN CALLED WOMEN "THE WEAKER SEX." A COMMON SAYING AT THE TIME WAS: "A WOMAN'S PLACE IS IN THE HOME." BUT BY THE 1960S AND 1970S, THINGS WERE

CHANGING. WOMEN WANTED THE SAME CAREERS
THAT MEN HAD—AS LAWYERS, DOCTORS, AIRPLANE
PILOTS, AND BUSINESS OWNERS. WOMEN WANTED
TO BE TREATED FAIRLY AT WORK, TO BE PAID THE
SAME AS MEN DOING THE SAME JOBS.

TO PROTEST THE PROBLEM, WOMEN MARCHED
IN THE STREETS. THERE WERE RALLIES FOR
WOMEN'S LIBERATION. GLORIA STEINEM, GERMAINE
GREER, AND OTHER FEMINISTS, AS THEY CALLED
THEMSELVES, WROTE BOOKS AND ARTICLES TO
MAKE PEOPLE THINK ABOUT THE ISSUE OF WOMEN'S
RIGHTS. OTHER WOMEN TALKED ABOUT BURNING
THEIR BRAS AS A SYMBOL OF FREEDOM.

SOCIETY CHANGED. NASA DID, TOO, AND BEGAN
TO SEEK OUT WOMEN AS ASTRONAUTS.

Sally's job interview lasted a week. First she was given a physical exam. Her hearing and vision were tested. She had to run on a treadmill to test her heart rate. She also had to spend time inside a round fabric-coated ball to prove she could handle being in a small, cramped space.

Sally was physically fit, and she was the right height, too. She was five feet five inches. Astronauts couldn't be too tall, or they wouldn't fit inside the space shuttle.

The physical tests weren't as important as the personal interviews. NASA asked Sally a lot of questions about her life. Two psychiatrists also talked to Sally to find out whether she was the right kind of person for the job. One was friendly and nice. The other was what Sally called "the bad guy psychiatrist, who tried to rattle you." But Sally Ride couldn't be rattled easily. She was always calm under pressure. Those were the qualities NASA wanted.

NASA was looking for people who were intelligent. Sally was certainly smart. She'd be able to handle tricky situations and solve problems that might come up during a spaceflight. NASA also wanted astronauts who were team players. Sally knew how to be part of a team from playing sports with boys.

During the interview, NASA told Sally that the training would take several years. She would have to work very hard. She would have to give up being an astrophysicist while learning to become an astronaut.

And after all the years of training, there was no guarantee that Sally would ever get to go into space!

Sally didn't mind any of that. She really wanted the job! After the interview, she flew home to California to wait. Months went by and she didn't hear anything. But finally, in January 1978, she got the call she had been hoping for. She had been picked to be one of NASA's thirty-five new astronauts!

In July 1978, she and the others in her class reported to Houston to begin training. They called themselves the Thirty-Five New Guys— or TFNG for short—even though Sally and five others were women.

BLUFORD

BRANDENSTEIN

BUCHLI

COATS

COVEY

CREIGHTON

FISHER

GARDNER

GIBSON

GREGORY

GRIGGS

HART

HAWLEY

HOFFMAN

LUCID

McBRIDE

McNAIR

MULLANE

NELSON

ONIZUKA

RESNIK

RIDE

SCOBEE

SEDDON

SHRIVER

STEWART

SULLIVAN

THAGARD

VAN HOFTEN

WALKER

FABIAN

HAUCK

NAGEL

SHAW

WILLIAMS

FIRST WOMAN IN SPACE

LONG BEFORE THE US EVER THOUGHT OF HAVING WOMEN ASTRONAUTS, THE SOVIET UNION SENT A WOMAN INTO SPACE. HER NAME WAS VALENTINA TERSESHKOVA. A FORMER FACTORY WORKER, VALENTINA WAS CHOSEN TO BE A COSMONAUT—THE RUSSIAN WORD FOR ASTRONAUT—PARTLY BECAUSE SHE WAS AN AMATEUR SKYDIVER.

VALENTINA FLEW IN A RUSSIAN SPACECRAFT IN 1963. SHE SPENT ALMOST THREE DAYS IN SPACE, CIRCLING THE EARTH FORTY-EIGHT TIMES. SHE BECAME A HEROINE TO THE RUSSIAN PEOPLE, REMEMBERED EVEN TODAY. LATER THAT YEAR, SHE MARRIED ANOTHER RUSSIAN COSMONAUT. WHEN THEY HAD A BABY GIRL, THEIR DAUGHTER WAS THE FIRST PERSON EVER BORN TO TWO PARENTS WHO HAD BOTH TRAVELED IN SPACE.

Chapter 4
Five Years of Hard Work

When Sally arrived in Houston for astronaut training, in some ways it felt like being back in school. The Johnson Space Center was laid out like a college campus. Many large buildings were connected by concrete walkways. One building was called Mission Control. This was where people on the ground directed flights in outer space. Other buildings held classrooms, offices, and labs.

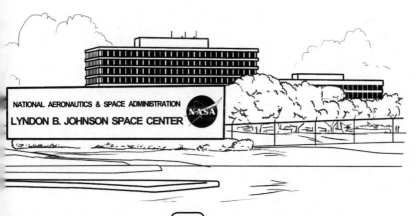

In her first year of training, Sally spent many hours sitting at a desk and studying. She had to learn everything about how the shuttle worked— the computers, the electrical systems, and the mechanical parts. Each astronaut had to know how to fix the shuttle if something went wrong in flight.

She also studied scientific subjects, like astronomy. She learned the locations of all the stars in the sky for navigation. She learned practical things like how to put on her space suit and how to survive in the water in case the space shuttle crashed in the ocean. She learned how to give first aid. She also learned how to do the other astronauts' jobs, in case someone got sick during a mission.

For the first year, Sally and the others in her class were called "astronaut candidates." That meant they were beginners. They hung out together and became friends. They shared pizza and beer at each other's houses. They were all competing for the chance to go into space, but it was a friendly competition.

The TFNG wouldn't be real, full-fledged astronauts until they learned everything they needed to know and passed a lot of tests.

Some of the tests were physical. Sally had to parachute out of planes and scuba dive in cold water. She had to spend time in a model of the shuttle called a simulator. It stayed on the ground. But it vibrated, turned her upside down, and played loud noises the whole time. It showed her what being in space would be like. She was also dropped into the ocean from forty feet in the air and then rescued by helicopter.

Another test was like a terrible, broken amusement park ride. Sally was strapped into a seat that zoomed along a track. At some point during the ride—she never knew when—she would be thrown from the seat and go flying through the air! The test proved that Sally could handle being ejected from a spacecraft in an emergency.

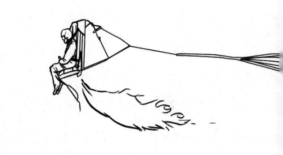

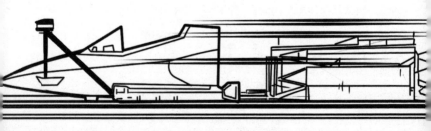

The hardest physical test was called "drop and drag." Sally was dropped in the water from a speeding boat, wearing her space suit and an open parachute. The parachute was still attached to the boat by a rope. Sally had to get out of the parachute harness while being dragged through the icy water. Then she had to swim to a dock a long way off. Surviving the "drop and drag" took all the strength she had.

In space, people are weightless. They float in the air. To practice being weightless, Sally took a special ride in a jet plane the astronauts called the "vomit comet." With several astronauts inside, the vomit comet climbed up through the sky in an arc. Then, all of a sudden, like a roller coaster, it dove down.

At the top of the arc, Sally and the other astronaut floated freely inside the cabin. They were weightless—but only for about thirty seconds! It wasn't exactly like being in outer space, but it gave Sally a taste of what it was like being weightless. She took over a thousand dives in the vomit comet before she ever rode the shuttle into space.

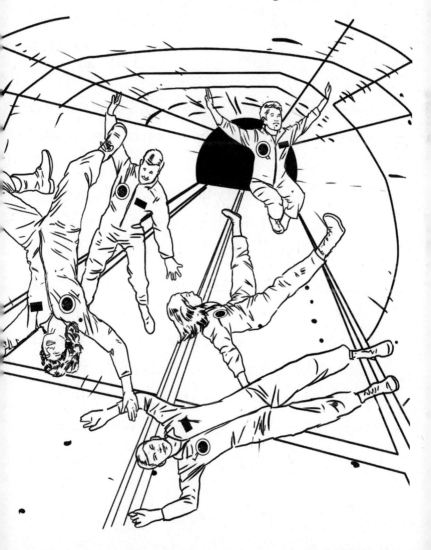

NASA wanted all the astronauts to stay in good physical shape, but they let each person decide how to do it. Sally chose to run several miles a day. She also lifted weights, so she would be strong enough to lift her forty-pound parachute.

Sally worked sixty hours a week on her training. That's like having one and a half full-time jobs. Sometimes she spent eight hours a day inside the cockpit of the shuttle simulator. There she learned how to read and react to all the cockpit controls. From time to time, NASA would create fake "emergencies." Sometimes all the power would go out, or the fuel would be low. Sally had to think fast, figuring out what to do.

She wasn't a pilot, and she didn't need to be

one. But she flew in a jet as part of her training. It turned out that she liked flying so much that she decided to get her pilot's license in her spare time.

In August 1979, Sally finished her first year of training. She and the TFNGs all became astronauts. Still, her training wasn't over.

Sally was called a mission specialist. It's the name for a scientist who has one or more special jobs to do on a spaceflight.

Sally's job was to help design a fifty-foot long robotic arm for the space shuttle. The robotic arm could lift things weighing more than thirty-two tons! It could lift heavy satellites out of the space shuttle's cargo area. Then the arm would send the satellite spinning off into space in the right direction. It could grab satellites from space and bring them back to Earth for repairs. The robotic arm could also be used to look at the outside of the space shuttle, to see if anything needed repair.

Sally spent two years working with the company that built the robotic arm. She also spent many hours practicing with it. Sally was the best person on her team at using the robotic arm, so she was chosen as the astronaut to use it for the first time in space.

Five long years went by as Sally waited for her turn to go up in space. The other TFNGs were waiting, too. One of them was a red-haired astronomer named Steve Hawley. He and Sally had become close friends—they had a lot in common. They both loved sports. They were both scientists who studied the stars. And they both wanted to go up into space as soon as possible.

Finally, in April 1982, Sally got the news that she had been chosen for a shuttle flight! She would be part of a crew that would fly a year later, in 1983. Steve Hawley, however, hadn't been chosen for a flight yet.

In July 1982, Sally and Steve got married. The small, private wedding was held at his parents' home in Kansas, where Steve had grown up. The ceremony was performed by two family members who were both ministers—Steve's father and Sally's sister, Bear. Sally flew a plane to the wedding, got married in blue jeans and a rugby shirt, and then flew straight back to Houston the same day—still waiting for the most important day in her life.

CAPCOM

DURING EVERY SPACEFLIGHT, THE ASTRONAUTS NEED TO SPEAK TO PEOPLE ON THE GROUND AT MISSION CONTROL. BUT MISSION CONTROL IS FILLED WITH DOZENS OF PEOPLE. IF THEY ALL TALKED AT ONCE, IT WOULD BE CHAOS. SO FOR EACH FLIGHT ONLY ONE PERSON IN HOUSTON IS CHOSEN TO SPEAK TO THE ASTRONAUTS. IN THE EARLY DAYS, ASTRONAUTS FLEW IN SPACE CAPSULES, SO THE PERSON IN HOUSTON WAS CALLED THE CAPCOM—SHORT FOR CAPSULE COMMUNICATOR. THE NICKNAME STUCK. THE ASTRONAUTS DON'T SAY

"HELLO, CAPCOM," THOUGH. THEY CALL THE CAPCOM "HOUSTON."

BEFORE EVER FLYING THE SHUTTLE HERSELF, SALLY RIDE WAS CHOSEN TO BE CAPCOM FOR TWO SHUTTLE FLIGHTS. THAT WAS AN HONOR. IT MEANT THAT NASA THOUGHT SALLY WAS DOING A GOOD JOB. IT ALSO HELPED HER UNDERSTAND WHAT HAPPENED ON THE GROUND DURING A SPACE-FLIGHT—USEFUL EXPERIENCE FOR WHEN SHE WOULD BE IN SPACE.

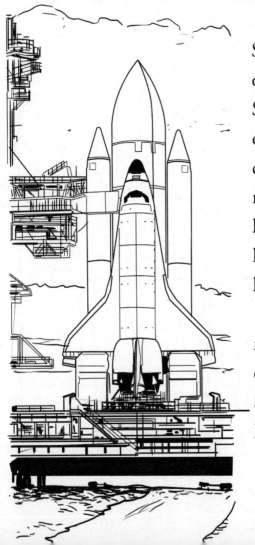

The big day for Sally finally arrived on June 18, 1983. She was going into outer space! Sally was chosen for a space mission before her husband, Steve. He had to wait a year longer for his turn.

It was early morning, still dark outside, when Sally arrived at the launchpad. All the

spaceflights were
launched from the
Kennedy Space Center in
Cape Canaveral, in Florida,
even though they were
controlled from Houston.
The weather in Florida was good
for most of the year. There would be fewer
cancelled liftoffs in a warm climate. Also,
Florida is right near the ocean. After a spacecraft
launched, the rockets could fall into the water
without hurting anyone on the ground. In early
spaceflights, the astronauts even landed in the
ocean in capsules when they returned to Earth.

In just a few hours, at 7:33 a.m., when the
space shuttle took off, Sally would become the
first American woman in space. For the next six
days, she would be inside the space shuttle, two
hundred miles from Earth. If everything went
well, she would return to Earth on June 24.

She had traveled to the launch with the four other astronauts in the crew. Bob Crippen was the commander—the pilot who was in charge of the

Norman Thagard

Frederick Hauck

Sally Ride

John Fabian

Robert Crippen

flight. Rick Hauck was also a pilot. John Fabian and Norm Thagard were mission specialists, just like Sally. They worked with the robotic arm. Norm Thagard was a medical doctor as well. On the trip, he would study how space travel affected the astronauts.

All five astronauts had been working together as a team for more than a year, so they were good friends.

As they stood at the bottom of the space shuttle *Challenger*, it towered above them. The shuttle, facing skyward with its huge fuel tank and two rockets, was close to thirty stories high. Sally and the others took an elevator up to a movable walkway that led them to the shuttle. They got on their helmets and climbed into their seats.

All the astronauts were facing the nose of the space shuttle, so they were lying on their backs. Sally was strapped in, ready to go. But still she had to wait almost an hour for liftoff.

Finally the launch engines ignited. Sally felt the whole shuttle shaking and vibrating with a tremendous power. She heard the roar of rocket engines so powerful that they could propel the huge, heavy shuttle into space in a few minutes.

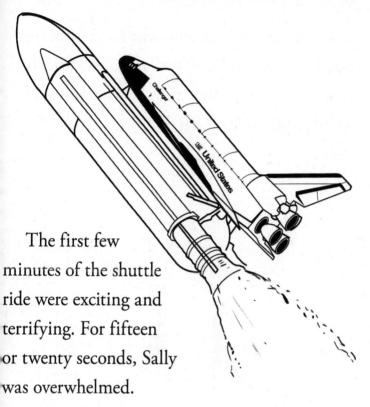

The first few
minutes of the shuttle
ride were exciting and
terrifying. For fifteen
or twenty seconds, Sally
was overwhelmed.
She said, "Every astronaut will tell you that launch
is just spectacular, exciting, petrifying, terrifying.
All those things."

As the shuttle climbed in the sky, the force of
gravity, called g-forces, pushed hard against her,
pinning her in her seat. She could barely move.
She wished this part of the flight would end soon.

The ride was quieter when the launch rockets stopped burning and dropped away. Soon the fuel tank would drop off, too, and the shuttle would be on its own, orbiting Earth.

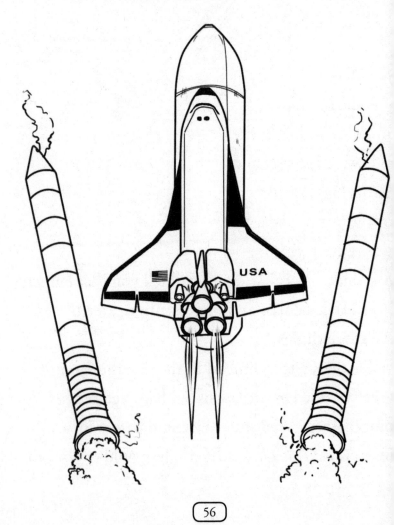

Finally, after eight and a half minutes, the shuttle reached outer space. Suddenly the force of gravity was gone. Sally was weightless!

She loved being weightless, and so did the other astronauts. As soon as the shuttle was safely in orbit, they began acting like five-year-old kids.

They watched their books and pencils float by.
They did somersaults in midair.

There was a lot of important work to do on the flight, so the astronauts quickly got busy. Sally used the robotic arm to launch a satellite. She had to release it at just the right moment. She spent a lot of time taking pictures for NASA, both inside the space shuttle and looking out. She also carried out other experiments. One experiment was a test

to see how ants in an ant colony would behave in space!

But when the astronauts weren't working, they had lots of fun.

During meals, they played with their food. Everything was weightless! They floated a cookie in midair and then "flew" an astronaut to catch it in his mouth. They floated peanuts across the cabin to each other. One time, an astronaut

floated a forkful of macaroni and cheese, and ate it from the fork without using his hands. Another astronaut even floated an orange drink in the air—without a container! The liquid stayed in a perfect ball in space. It didn't splatter or crash to the floor since there was no gravity.

It was the most fun Sally had ever had in her life.

Being weightless was tricky, though. Sally had to learn how to move around the cabin, pushing off from the walls. If she pushed too hard, she crashed into the opposite wall.

She had to learn how to bend over gently and put on her socks. If she wasn't careful, she would just start spinning head over heels in slow motion.

Sally wore loose, regular clothes in space. She only needed her space suit for the launch and landing. Shoes were pointless—she didn't walk on the floor! Besides, it was too dangerous to wear shoes. If she floated near another astronaut, she might accidentally kick him in the head.

Using the bathroom was different in space. There was no sink because there was no running water. Water from a faucet would have just floated around in the shuttle in drops! Instead, Sally squirted water onto a cloth from a water gun and washed her face. To use the toilet, she had to strap her legs down so she wouldn't float away. Then she turned on an air-suction hose. It sucked the body wastes away.

VELCRO

UNTIL NASA PUT VELCRO TO USE IN EARLY SPACEFLIGHTS, NO ONE IN AMERICA HAD HEARD OF IT.

VELCRO WAS INVENTED BY A SWISS ENGINEER NAMED GEORGES DE MESTRAL IN THE 1940S. HE NOTICED THAT WHEN HE WALKED IN THE WOODS WITH HIS DOG, BURRS STUCK TO HIS DOG'S COAT. THE BURRS GAVE THE ENGINEER AN IDEA. WHAT IF THERE WAS A WAY TO MAKE THINGS STICK TOGETHER AND THEN COME APART EASILY, JUST LIKE THE BURRS?

THE MAN SPENT TEN YEARS TRYING TO INVENT VELCRO. IN THE 1950S HE FINALLY SUCCEEDED. BUT VELCRO DIDN'T CATCH ON RIGHT AWAY. PEOPLE THOUGH IT WAS UGLY AND IMPRACTICAL.

NASA THOUGHT IT WAS PRETTY COOL, THOUGH. VELCRO MADE IT EASIER FOR ASTRONAUTS TO GET IN AND OUT OF THEIR SPACE SUITS. IT WAS ALSO PERFECT FOR SPACEFLIGHT. WITH VELCRO, THE ASTRONAUTS COULD ATTACH FOOD TRAYS TO THEIR PANTS, SO THE TRAYS WOULDN'T FLOAT AWAY IN SPACE.

THE ASTRONAUTS USED VELCRO FOR EVERYTHING. THEY USED IT TO STICK THEIR TOOLS TO THEIR UNIFORMS. THEY USED IT TO STICK

FOOD POUCHES OR CAMERAS TO THE WALLS OF THE SPACE SHUTTLE.

WHEN AMERICANS LEARNED THAT THE ASTRONAUTS WERE USING VELCRO, IT BECAME MORE POPULAR. NOW VELCRO IS EVERYWHERE— IN SPACE AND ON EARTH. YOU PROBABLY HAVE SOME ON YOUR JACKET, BACKPACK, SLEEPING BAG, OR RUNNING SHOES. NASA DIDN'T INVENT VELCRO, BUT THEY TURNED IT INTO A BIG SUCCESS.

Day and night were strange in space because the sun was constantly coming up and going down. That's because the space shuttle circled the Earth sixteen times every twenty-four hours. Sally saw the sun rise and set every ninety minutes!

When it was time to sleep, Sally climbed into a thin sleeping bag and just floated near a window. She loved to look out at the Earth from space.

Sally could see the thin layer of Earth's atmosphere. That layer of gases is what lets us breathe on Earth. It keeps our planet warm. From space, the layer looked like a thin blue line. Sally thought a lot about how fragile our Earth is, how little separates us from the coldness of outer space, and how important it was to protect our atmosphere from harm.

After six days in space, it was time to go home. The mission had been a big success. The shuttle had carried more astronauts than ever before. All the satellites had been launched properly. Nothing had gone wrong.

But first, the astronauts had to clean up the space shuttle. All kinds of things were floating around the cabin—bits of hair, food crumbs, pencils that had drifted away during the flight. If they didn't find all the loose items and put them away, all those things would come crashing down on them during the re-entry to Earth. And if they didn't clean up the floating crumbs, they might clog up the complicated computers on board.

It took the astronauts two hours to get dressed for the return flight. Sally put on her space suit— but she couldn't find her boots! She almost had to go back to Earth in her socks. Finally she found her boots, just in time.

HOW HIGH IS UP?

WHERE DOES OUTER SPACE BEGIN?

SURPRISINGLY, OUTER SPACE BEGINS ONLY ABOUT FIFTY MILES ABOVE THE SURFACE OF THE EARTH. IF THERE WERE A HIGHWAY GOING STRAIGHT UP, YOU COULD DRIVE YOUR CAR TO OUTER SPACE IN LESS THAN AN HOUR!

MOST AIRPLANES FLY ABOUT SIX MILES ABOVE THE EARTH. THE SPACE SHUTTLE FLEW TO ABOUT TWO HUNDRED MILES ABOVE THE EARTH, AND THEN BEGAN ORBITING. SATELLITES ARE MUCH FARTHER AWAY, THOUGH. THEY

CAN CIRCLE THE EARTH FROM 22,000 MILES HIGH!

WHEN ASTRONAUTS LANDED ON THE MOON, THEY WERE ALMOST A QUARTER OF A MILLION MILES AWAY. FROM THE MOON, THEY COULD SEE THE WHOLE EARTH. IT LOOKED LIKE A BIG BLUE-AND-WHITE MARBLE. BUT IN THE SPACE SHUTTLE, THE ASTRONAUTS WEREN'T THAT FAR AWAY. WHEN SALLY RIDE LOOKED AT THE EARTH FROM SPACE, SHE COULD ONLY SEE A BIG SECTION OF OUR PLANET AND THE CURVE OF THE EARTH, PROTECTED BY THAT THIN BLUE LINE THAT IS THE EARTH'S ATMOSPHERE.

Strapped into her seat, Sally watched as the space shuttle re-entered Earth's atmosphere. Once the shuttle was near the Earth, it flew like a glider.

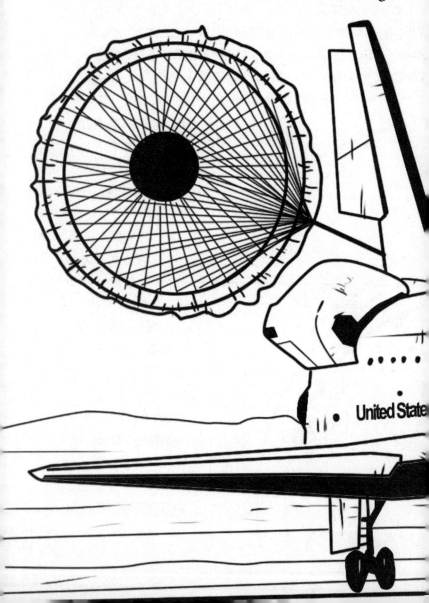

There were no engines controlling the speed—the shuttle was just falling toward Earth, pulled by gravity. It glided and swooped in different directions to slow down. The movements were controlled by computers, and then by the pilot.

When they landed on a runway in California, the shuttle was still going two hundred miles an hour. A huge parachute opened at the back of the shuttle to help slow it down and then stop.

Now that the shuttle had stopped, the astronauts could get out of their seats. But Sally could barely move! Her arms and legs felt heavy after days in weightless space. She could barely stand up or walk in a straight line. She was dizzy, and her heart was racing. She tried to lift her boots, but it felt like there were lead weights inside them.

It took about thirty minutes before she and the other astronauts felt normal again. When they could walk and climb down steps without staggering, they were allowed to leave the shuttle.

Sally had just had the best experience of her whole life. But she had no idea what was waiting for her outside.

Chapter 6
Being Sally Ride

Sally was thrilled and excited to have ridden the shuttle. She was proud to be an astronaut. But she didn't want to make a big deal about being the first woman in space. Like the men on her mission, she was smart, strong, coolheaded and hardworking. She didn't think it should matter whether she was a woman or a man.

But the rest of the world saw it differently. People in America were fascinated by Sally. An old rock-and-roll song called "Mustang Sally" became popular again. The song wasn't originally about Sally Ride, but the lyrics said, "Ride, Sally, ride." People wore T-shirts with "Ride, Sally Ride" printed on them.

TV and newspaper reporters wanted to talk to

her. Her picture was on the cover of magazines.
NASA sent her to speak to people all over
America.

Sally didn't like doing interviews. She had
always been very private, almost shy. And she
didn't like being treated differently from the male
astronauts. The questions were insulting! Before
her first trip into space, a reporter had asked her

if she would cry when things went wrong. Sally laughed at the question, but she didn't think it was funny. After six months crisscrossing America, she told NASA that she didn't want to do any more publicity tours.

For the next few months, Sally spent time getting ready for her next space-shuttle flight.

Meanwhile, her husband, Steve Hawley, had also been chosen for a mission, but not the same one as Sally's. He rode the space shuttle *Discovery* in August 1984.

Two months later, in October, Sally took her second shuttle trip in *Challenger*. This time there were seven astronauts on board—including another woman, Kathryn Sullivan.

One day, Sally and Kathryn Sullivan were sitting around talking. Somehow they started talking about their childhoods. It turned out that they had both gone to the same elementary school! No one at NASA realized it, but they had been in first grade together.

Sally's second spaceflight was very different from her first. Many things went a little bit wrong. When Sally tried to launch a satellite, she found that some of the hinges were frozen. The satellite wouldn't work properly. Thinking quickly, she asked the pilot to turn the space shuttle toward the sun. With the cargo-bay doors open, the sun shone on the satellite and thawed the hinges. Every day brought a new problem. One day, an antenna on the shuttle didn't work. Another day, a radar panel wouldn't close. But Sally didn't panic—and she certainly didn't cry! She calmly used the robotic arm to fix the panel.

She was great at solving problems. That's why NASA had chosen her.

This time when Sally came back to Earth, she was not famous for being a woman. She was just famous for being an astronaut. She liked it that way—and couldn't wait to go up in space again.

Chapter 7
Tragedy in Space

On January 28, 1986, the whole world was watching as the space shuttle *Challenger* prepared to launch from Cape Canaveral. This launch was especially exciting because an ordinary high-school teacher was going along on the trip. Christa McAuliffe, the teacher, had trained for a year to be the first teacher in space. Schools all over

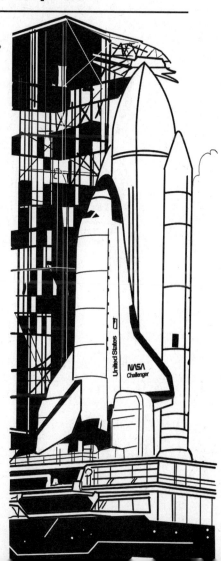

America were watching the launch on TV, waiting to see what a teacher would say about spaceflight.

Sally Ride was not among the astronauts on this flight, which began on a sunny but very cold day. The launch appeared to go all right. Then, just a little more than a minute later, something terrible happened. The shuttle's fuel tanks leaked, creating a huge burst of fire and smoke. Then the shuttle itself broke into pieces. All seven of the astronauts on board the *Challenger* died. It was a tragedy for the whole country.

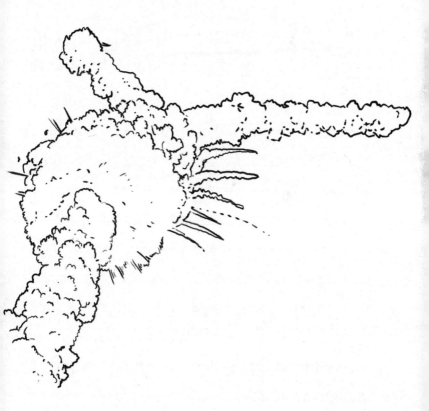

Sally Ride was driving to the Johnson Space Center in Houston, listening to her car radio. When she heard the horrible news, she couldn't believe it. All the astronauts on board were her very close friends. She had known them for years and worked with them every day. She knew their families. She had spent time at their homes.

Everyone was shocked and stunned by the disaster. NASA knew that there could be no more space-shuttle flights until they found out what had gone wrong.

Sally was supposed to go up in the shuttle just two months later, but now that was out of the question. NASA cancelled the flight.

Instead, President Ronald Reagan asked Sally to help investigate the *Challenger* accident. Together with other scientists, businessmen, and politicians, Sally spent four months trying to find out what had happened to the *Challenger*.

It turned out that several things had gone wrong. First there was the problem with the O-rings on the rockets. O-rings are sort of like the rubber rings that keep liquids from leaking out of a blender. They should have kept the rockets sealed tight so fuel wouldn't leak out, but they didn't.

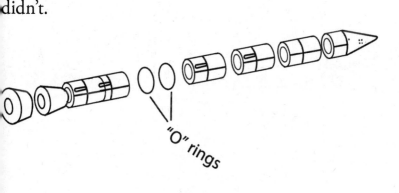

"O" rings

ROGER BOISJOLY:
WHISTLEBLOWER

ONE MAN TRIED TO STOP THE *CHALLENGER* FROM LAUNCHING ON THAT TERRIBLE DAY.

HIS NAME WAS ROGER BOISJOLY, AND HE WORKED FOR THE COMPANY THAT MADE THE SHUTTLE'S ROCKETS. ROGER KNEW THE O-RINGS MIGHT NOT WORK PROPERLY. HE TRIED TO TELL HIS BOSSES, BUT THEY DIDN'T WANT TO LISTEN. THEY WANTED TO KEEP NASA HAPPY—AND NASA WANTED THE SHUTTLE LAUNCH TO GO AHEAD.

AFTER THE *CHALLENGER* DISASTER, ROGER BOISJOLY WAS ASKED QUESTIONS ABOUT WHAT HAPPENED. HE SPOKE IN FRONT OF THE COMMITTEE THAT THE GOVERNMENT SET UP. HE TOLD THE TRUTH. AFTERWARD, ROGER'S BOSSES AND HIS COWORKERS WERE MAD AT HIM FOR GETTING THE COMPANY IN TROUBLE. NASA WAS UNHAPPY ABOUT IT, TOO. BUT SALLY RIDE WALKED RIGHT UP TO HIM IN FRONT OF EVERYONE AND GAVE HIM A HUG. SHE KNEW HE HAD DONE THE RIGHT THING BY "BLOWING THE WHISTLE" ON HIS BOSSES AND NASA.

Second, the weather was too cold for a space launch. Cold weather meant the O-rings were more likely to harden and then leak.

But the biggest problem was that NASA made bad decisions that day. There were warnings about the O-rings before the launch. NASA went ahead with the mission anyway.

Sally was angry when she found out the truth. Her friends didn't have to die. The shuttle program needed to change—and Sally was going to make sure that happened.

Chapter 8
Starting Over

After the *Challenger* disaster, Sally decided to change her life. She simply didn't want to go up into space again—not right away, at least. It seemed too dangerous, and besides, NASA didn't want anyone to fly for the next few years, until it was safe.

Sally had other reasons for making a change, too. She had always loved science and wanted to go back to being a physicist. If she didn't do it soon, she would lose her chance.

Sally's last reason for making a change was very personal. Sally wanted to end her marriage, so she could be with Tam O'Shaughnessy. Sally had known Tam since their early days of playing tennis together. Sally and Tam were in love with

each other. Sally and Steve Hawley got divorced in 1987. Sally was with Tam for the rest of her life.

There was an important job to do before Sally left NASA. She spent almost a year working on a report about safety and the space program, and what should be done in the future. When the report was done, it became known as the Ride Report, because Sally was the leader on the project.

The Ride Report said that the US should try to do four things. First, NASA should send satellites into space to keep watch on Earth. If our environment was being harmed, the satellites would show that. Sally was still thinking about that thin layer of Earth's atmosphere, and how fragile it was. Secondly, NASA should send unmanned spacecraft (ones with no people aboard) to nearby planets like Mars. Even though Mars is the closest planet to Earth, it still takes almost a year to get there—and a year to get back! It would be safer to send a spacecraft without people on board. Third, would it be possible to create a permanent space station on the moon? And fourth, what would it take to send a manned mission to Mars?

Sally's most important recommendation,

though, was that the government should make sure NASA had enough money for space travel to be as safe as possible.

When the Ride Report was complete, Sally resigned from NASA. Then she moved back to California to be with Tam, and to start a new life as a professor.

Chapter 9
Science Is for Girls

For the next two years, Sally worked at Stanford University as a scientist. Then she moved to the University of California, San Diego, where she became the director of the California Space Institute.

But all this time, another career idea was beginning to bubble up in Sally's mind. She was starting to think about how to help girls do well in science, so they might have careers like her own.

All her life, Sally had been determined to be treated like "just one of the boys." But as she traveled around the country and spoke to schoolchildren, she realized that being a *female* astronaut—not just an astronaut—was

a good thing. Girls looked up to her. They felt encouraged by the fact that she did a job that only men had done before. And she did it really well!

Sally also noticed something odd. Girls loved science and math when they were in elementary school. But by high school things changed. Older girls sometimes fell behind in those subjects. Sally thought she knew how to help.

Sally had already written a book for children about her spaceflight, *To Space and Back*. But were there other ways to excite kids, especially girls, about science and math?

Sally's first project for kids was called KidSat, and it was a project she developed with help from NASA. The project allowed students at three different schools to come up with science experiments to be carried out during space-shuttle missions. One of the projects involved a camera mounted on the space shuttle's flight deck. The students were allowed to control the camera themselves, from school, while the shuttle was in space!

Eventually, in 2001, Sally started her own company called Sally Ride Science. Sally was the chief executive officer of the company. Her partner in the project was Tam. Tam had always loved science. One of her favorite memories as a child was watching tadpoles in a creek as they changed into frogs. Sally and Tam had also written several science books together. Now they were working side by side to create programs that would inspire young students, especially girls, to hold on to their love of science and pursue scientific careers.

Sally Ride
Science

For the next eleven years, Sally continued to do all those things. She was a scientist, a former astronaut, and the head of her own company. She also received many honors and awards. In 2003, she was voted into the Astronaut Hall of Fame. More than five hundred astronauts had flown in

space, but only forty-eight of them had received that honor at the time Sally and two others were inducted that year.

On July 23, 2012, Sally Ride died at her home in San Diego at the age of sixty-one. The world was shocked to find out that she had been fighting cancer for more than a year. The world was also surprised to learn that Sally was gay. Always very private, Sally had told only her close family and friends about her illness, and about her relationship with Tam. She did not want the public to know about this part of her life until after she'd died. Some wished Sally had been more open about being gay. But that wasn't Sally's way. She had never liked labels. And she had never wanted a bright light shone on her private life. She wanted her work and her accomplishments to speak for themselves. She wanted to be remembered, as President Reagan said when she first went up into space, as having been chosen because she was "the best person for the job."

Most of all, Sally wanted kids to do as she had done, and follow the advice she gave at the end of every talk. She wanted young students to "Reach for the stars."

TIMELINE OF
SALLY RIDE'S LIFE

1951 — Born in Encino, California, on May 26

1960 — Her family spends a year traveling Europe

1968 — Graduates from Westlake School for Girls

1970 — Drops out of Swarthmore College to pursue tennis

1973 — Graduates with bachelor's degrees in physics and Englis
from Stanford University

1975 — Receives her master's degree in physics from Stanford
University

1977 — Applies to be an astronaut at NASA

1978 — Receives her PhD in physics from Stanford University
Selected by NASA to be an astronaut candidate
Begins four years of training, during which she designs
fifty-foot-long robotic arm

1982 — Marries Steve Hawley

1983 — Becomes the first American woman to fly in space aboa
the *Challenger* on June 18

1984 — Takes her second trip aboard the *Challenger*

1986 — The *Challenger* explodes on January 28
Appointed to the committee investigating the disaster
Publishes *To Space and Back*

1987 — Retires from NASA
Divorces Steve Hawley to live with Tam O'Shaughness

2001 — Founds Sally Ride Science for elementary- and middle-
school students

2003 — Inducted into the Astronaut Hall of Fame

2012 — Dies on July 23

TIMELINE OF THE WORLD

iss inventor Georges de Mestral formally patents Velcro	1955
The National Aeronautics and Space Administration (NASA) is founded	1958
Russian Yuri Gagarin becomes the first human to fly in space	1961
ssian Valentina Tereshkova becomes the first woman to fly in space Betty Friedan's *The Feminine Mystique is published*	1963
Wilson Pickett releases the song "Mustang Sally"	1966
Dr. Martin Luther King Jr. is shot and killed in April	1968
Armstrong, commander of *Apollo 11*, steps foot on the moon The Woodstock Festival takes place	1969
The first electronic book is invented The floppy disk is introduced	1971
The Vietnam War ends	1975
a Day O'Connor becomes the first female US Supreme Court Judge	1981
Dolly the sheep is the first successfully cloned animal Tiger Woods wins his first PGA Tour event	1996
September 11, the terrorist group al-Qaeda flies planes he Twin Towers in New York City and the Pentagon in Washington, DC	2001
arack Obama becomes the first African American to be elected president of the US	2008
aeda leader Osama bin Laden is killed in Pakistan by a team of US Navy Seals	2011

BIBLIOGRAPHY

*Camp, Carole Ann. **Sally Ride: First American Woman in Space**. Springfield, NJ: Enslow Publishers, 1997.*

*Hurwitz, Jane, and Sue Hurwitz. **Sally Ride: Shooting for the Stars**. New York: Fawcett Books, 1989.

*Kramer, Barbara. **Sally Ride: A Space Biography**. Springfield, NJ: Enslow Publishers, 1998.

*Riddolls, Tom. **Sally Ride: The First American Woman in Space**. New York: Crabtree Publishing, 2011.

*Ride, Sally, and Susan Okie. **To Space and Back**. New York: Beech Tree, 1986.

VIDEO DOCUMENTARY: **The Sally Ride Story: A Woman Space Pioneer**. DVD. Beverly Hills: Global Science Productions, 2000.

*For young readers

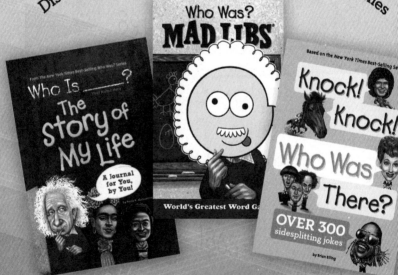